SHOW ME HOW

Knitting
to the rescue!

A Story About
Learning to Knit

Susan Levin and Gloria Tracy

sixth&spring books

We dedicate our *Show Me How* books to our mothers, Ruth Straumer Wagner and Mary Bridges Jensma. They inspired us to find a lifetime of pleasure, creative outlets and contentment in a wide range of crafts. We think they would be pleased to see another generation of budding crafters being inspired to carry on the tradition.

— SL and GT

Editorial Director: Elaine Silverstein

Book Division Manager: Erica Smith

Associate Editor: Amanda Keiser

Story Written By: Cherie Troped

Vice President, Publisher: Trisha Malcolm

Production Manager: David Joinnides

Copy Editor: Kristina Sigler

Art Director, Project Manager: Nancy Sabato

Illustrations: Cathi Mingus

Creative Director: Joe Vior

President, Sixth&Spring Books: Art Joinnides

Library of Congress Control Number: 2007921002

ISBN: 1-933027-27-4

ISBN-13: 978-1-933027-27-2

Manufactured in China

1 3 5 7 9 10 8 6 4 2

First Edition

chapter one

"**M**ary Ruth! Jacob! If we don't leave for Grandma's house this very minute, we're going to be late!" my mom yelled.

My mom is always worried about being late. And I'm kind of like her. I always think if I'm one second late for school it will be absolutely the most horrible thing in the world – that it will go on my permanent record *permanently*.

My brother, Jacob is another story. He's always late. But then, he's a boy.

Jacob and I are going to stay at Grandma's house because my dad is running a marathon this weekend and my mom is going to cheer him on.

Jacob likes to go to Grandma's house because she still has the basketball hoop that my uncle used when he was a kid. He also loves the cookies that she bakes for us.

Jacob ran down the stairs carrying what looked like a whole electronics store. "Okay," he said. "Laptop computer . . . check, video games . . . check, music player . . . check, cell phone . . . check, DVD player . . . check. Okay, I'm packed. Let's go."

"I can't believe you're taking all that, that *equipment* to Grandma's. Aren't you going to spend time with her?" I asked him.

"Well, sure. I mean when I'm eating cookies and stuff. But listen, Mary Ruth, I'm up to the seventh level of this really hot video game and if I want to be a grandmaster, I gotta keep my digits movin'."

"I don't have a clue about what you're saying," I told him.

"Look," he said. "This is all important stuff that I need. I can't be away from any of it for a whole weekend. Girls just don't understand anything."

I was busy trying to get my stuff together, too. Especially the most important item of all — my cat, Phoebe. Phoebe is the best cat in the world.

She likes to play and purr and when she curls up in a ball in your lap, it is the best feeling in the world. I had to make sure she had enough food for the weekend plus her catnip mouse, her brush and her Kitty Cookies.

"If you two are ready, I'll just back the moving van up to the door and we can go," said my mom. She was kidding, I think. But we did have a lot of stuff. In addition to Phoebe and all of her equipment, I had clothes, books, my sketchpad and colored pencils and some more books.

Jacob was pretty quiet on the ride up to Grandma's. He had his music plugged into his ear while he was playing with his video game.

"We are going to have so much fun at Grandma's," I tried to yell over his music player.

"Yeah, yeah, whatever," he said, ignoring me.

chapter two

I was really looking forward to spending time with Grandma. She is sooooo cool. She lives in this really old house with a real front porch. And even though she does have normal 21st century things, she likes her house to look like it did when it was built at the start of the 20th century. It's like stepping back into a time machine. And that is totally fun.

It's really old fashioned, but in a good way. She has cordless phones but she also has this majorly old phone with a *dial*. She has a color TV and a *black and white* set.

What's really awesome is that my Grandma has a craft room! That's what I love. Last time I talked to Grandma she promised to show me something special over the weekend. And when I asked her what it was, she wouldn't tell me.

"A surprise is a surprise," she said.

Grandma was standing on the front porch when we drove up.

"You look so beautiful!" she said with a smile.

"Thank you!" I answered.

"I wasn't talking to you, Mary Ruth, I was talking to Phoebe." Then she laughed and gave me a big hug. "You're all beautiful. Come here, Jacob. You have to get your required hug from Grandma," she said, opening her arms to Jacob, who was still attached to his music player and video game.

"Hi, Grandma," he said as he let her hug him. "Is there an outlet I can use to hook up my laptop and charge my cell phone battery?"

"I think I can find one for you," Grandma said. "But don't you want some milk and cookies first?"

"Actually, Grandma, I need to charge my batteries first. I'll do a cookie later," Jacob said.

"I'll do a cookie NOW, please," I said to Grandma. "If 'doing a cookie' means eating one, that is."

The cookies were great, but I couldn't wait for Grandma's surprise. I knew she had something special planned. But what was it?

phoebe followed us into the kitchen. Phoebe ate her Kitty Cookies and Grandma and I sat down at the old wooden table to talk. "Grandma," I said. "I'm sorry if Jacob was rude. He's like that to all of us. I think it's because he's almost a teenager and they are weird."

"I know," said Grandma. "He's growing up and he thinks that if something isn't connected to an electrical cord, it isn't any good."

"Or a battery," I said.

"A cord and batteries," said Grandma. "I stand corrected."

So there we were all cozy in the kitchen with Phoebe sleeping on Grandma's lap, making little purring sounds in her sleep, when it started to rain.

Grandma looked out the window. "Uh oh, this looks like it's going to be a big storm."

Just then we heard the thunder.

Which was quickly followed by lightning.

Which was quickly followed by darkness because all the lights in the house went out.

"Jacob, are you okay up there?" yelled Grandma. Jacob always liked to stay in the attic room. "Come down to the kitchen. We saved a cookie for you."

"Hey, what happened?" he asked. "I was watching a DVD and everything went black. Can you call someone to turn the power back on?"

"We're having a big storm," said Grandma. "And when we have storms here, the electricity tends to go out. Especially in this old house."

"Boy, am I glad I charged my batteries," he said plopping down in a kitchen chair.

"Me, too!" said Grandma with a smile.

Before it got completely dark, Grandma got some candles out and we lit them. She even had some kerosene lanterns. "This was what people used before electricity," she said. "We'll have a cold, candlelit supper tonight and hopefully the electricity will be back on sometime tomorrow."

"Tomorrow?" cried Jacob. "What are we going to do 'til tomorrow?"

"We'll play games by candlelight tonight and hopefully the electricity will be back on tomorrow when I show Mary Ruth her surprise," said Grandma with a smile.

When it was time for bed we climbed the stairs and settled into our rooms. I always stay in my mom's old room. I love to sleep under her soft, cozy quilts. And I like to imagine what it was like growing up in that big old house and what she was like when she was my age.

chapter four

The next day was still stormy, and the electricity was still out. And Jacob's batteries were wearing down.

"Jacob, would you like to bring your computer game downstairs?" my Grandma called up to Jacob.

"Sure, I guess so," he said. "It's really dark up here," he yelled from his attic room. "Besides, my batteries are dying."

"Let's go into the craft room," Grandma said.

"With all the windows, the light is good in there and I can show you the surprise I have planned for you, Mary Ruth — and you too, Jacob."

"Great!" I said. "I can't wait."

"Oh, boy," said Jacob sarcastically. "This will be so exciting."

My Grandma's craft room is the best place in the world. She has everything in there — yarn, ribbons, fabric, scraps of lace, different kinds of paper, buttons, and well, just stuff for all kinds of projects that she works on. She makes everything from patchwork quilts to beautiful memory books. She knows how to knit and crochet and she does needlepoint and embroidery. She even makes things like shadow boxes and birdhouses. She's very creative.

And she says that I take right after her . . . which means that I am a lot like her. I guess that's because she and I have the same name. I never think that Grandma has another name but her real name is Ruth.

The Mary part came from my other grandma.

I couldn't wait to see what Grandma's surprise was.

"Mary Ruth , remember how you told me that
Phoebe loves to sleep on your favorite sweater?"

"Yes. It's my pink and purple one with the stripes. She sleeps on it all the time."

"Well, what if we made Phoebe a nice sweater of her own?"

"Grandma, Phoebe doesn't need a sweater. She has a big thick fur coat," I said.

"No, not for her to wear — for her to sleep on. A little comforter just for her. I'm going to teach you how to knit one."

"That sounds hard," I said. "I don't know how to knit."

"It's not hard at all," Grandma said. "Here, I'll show you."

I had to admit that making Phoebe her own comforter sounded like a good plan. I would learn to knit and Phoebe would finally give me back my favorite sweater.

Grandma went to the cupboard and found some beautiful yarn and knitting needles.

"We're just going to make a couple of rectangles," she said. "It's a lot of fun."

"I could make a little comforter for my dolls, too," I said. "Or one for our neighbor's new baby."

chapter five

In the soft light of the craft room, with the sound of the rain making gentle noises on the roof, Grandma took the yarn and a pair of knitting needles and we started to make Phoebe's kitty comforter.

Jacob stared out the window. "I'm bored," he said in his really grumpy voice. "What am I supposed to do while you do this girly stuff?"

"Lots of men knit, Jacob. I can teach you too. It's a good thing to know."

"Yeah, right. All the guys knit in my school. Not!" Jacob grumbled.

"Did you know that until the Industrial Revolution men were the *only* ones allowed to knit?"

"Uh, no! But what am I supposed to make? *A kitty comforter*?" he said making little quote marks around the words kitty comforter.

Grandma said. "I think Phoebe will have plenty with the ones Mary Ruth will make for her. But there are lots of other things you can make from a square or rectangle," Grandma said.

"You could knit Barkley a dog toy," I said.

"Yeah, like I could knit a ball," said Jacob.

"Actually, that's not a bad idea," Grandma said. "It's almost the same pattern as the one I'm showing Mary Ruth. And I'm sure that I have something around the house you could fill it with. I think Barkley would like that a lot."

Now if there was one thing that my brother loved that wasn't battery operated or electronic, it was our

dog, Barkley. They were the best of friends. Of course Barkley is a friend to everyone . . . even Phoebe. It's not true that cats and dogs don't get along. Sometimes they get along better than brothers and sisters.

"Yeah, I guess I could do that," he said. Barkley was staying with his best dog friend at our next-door neighbor's house, along with our little brother Justin.

So it was in Grandma's craft room that my techno-brother Jacob picked up a pair of knitting needles and started making a ball for Barkley.

I have to admit that the afternoon in my Grandma's pretty craft room, with no electricity and a big storm raging outside, was one of the happiest times of my life . . . so far.

And I will always remember the sight of my big brother sitting with a pair of knitting needles making a ball for good ol' Barkley. He was actually having fun — without batteries.

And Phoebe is going to love, love, love her comforter because I love, love, love knitting! It is so much fun, and easy, too!

If you would like to learn how to knit, I can show you how. I wrote down the directions just the way Grandma taught me.